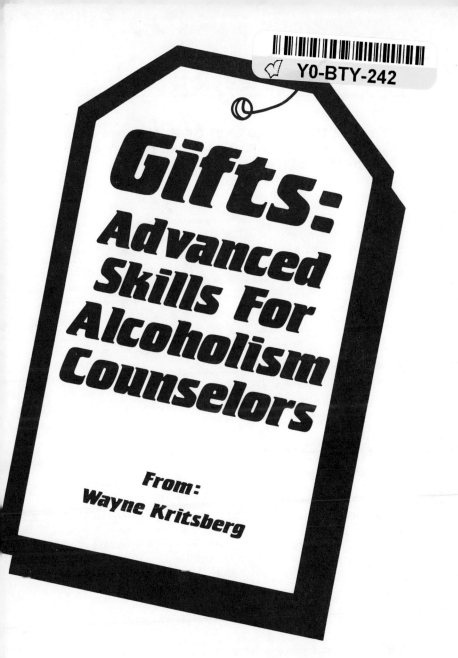

Gifts:
Advanced Skills For Alcoholism Counselors

From:
Wayne Kritsberg

The personal examples used in this book are based on my experiences as an alcoholism counselor. In all cases involving quotations from client histories, I have either used composites of several different people, or changed the clients' names. This was done to ensure privacy and confidentiality.

Dedication

I dedicate this book to all of those who have shared themselves with me, and who, in their turn, have allowed me to share myself with them.

Published by: Health Communications, Inc.
                  1721 Blount Road, Suite 1
                  Pompano Beach, FL 33069

Printed in the United States of America

ISBN: 0-932194-18-4

Table of Contents

Acknowledgments

There were many people who encouraged me to write this book, and who have given me encouragement during the actual process of writing it. To all these people I wish to express my deepest appreciation and thanks; without their support this project would have been much more difficult. There are, however, four people whom I wish to acknowledge for their special contributions to this endeavor:

Jan Christie: For her artwork.

Phil Orrick: His friendship and support were invaluable to this project. When I needed to get a refill on my enthusiasm, all I had to do was go to Phil and get some of his.

Susan Chiddix: Her loving support and encouragement during the day-to-day process of writing this book really made a difference. Without her the road would have been much bumpier.

Annemarie Micklo: Her many hours of editorial guidance are but a small part of her contribution to this book. Her love, encouragement, ideas, and hard work made this book happen.

Thank you very much.

Introduction

There is a power in each one of us that heals. This healing power is not normally accessible to us. Somehow, as we move through the day-to-day process of our lives, we lose the knowledge that we have the gift of self-healing. For whatever reason, we repress our birthright of self-forgiveness and self-love.

Counseling is the art of assisting a person back to an awareness of his own healing power. We, the counselors, cannot heal our clients (as much as we may want to). What we can do, however, is provide our clients with the tools and the space so that they can begin the process of healing themselves. This is what this book is about: making available to our clients some of the tools of self-healing and self-discovery.

As Alcoholism Counselors, we dip into the process of our clients' lives on an infrequent basis —for an hour or so once a week. Those of us who are counselors at treatment programs may see a client several times a week, either individually or in group, but then the client leaves treatment and we generally lose contact with him. The fact is, over an extended period of time, most of us see our clients infrequently. In order to maximize our effectiveness with our clients, using the limited amount of time that we have, it is necessary that we, the counselors, share techniques with them that they can take from the counseling experience—practical techniques that they can use in their daily lives. These techniques will enrich the clients' lives, and provide them with the means to work through difficult issues that they encounter, either from the past, or in the day-to-day process of living.

The skills and techniques that are discussed in this book are not intended to replace the traditional counseling methods that have proven effective in counseling the alcoholic client. There are many good books about counseling. This book is directed toward the counselor who already has a solid basis in counseling skills, but would like to enhance and enlarge his client's role in the therapeutic process.

These techniques can be effectively used by the client, to accelerate and enhance his own growth. They are, in my experience, most effective when used with clients who have been alcohol- and drug-free for a period of time, although each client will be ready to learn and accept these tools at a different point in his recovery.

These techniques are tools that can be given to your client, tools that he can work with in the day-to-day process of living. These tools are powerful and they do work. The beauty of them is that once the client learns to use them, he has them at his disposal for the rest of his life.

There is an old Chinese proverb that goes:

Give a man a fish and you feed him for a day.
Teach a man to fish and you feed him for a lifetime.

This is what these tools are all about. They are techniques that you can give to your client that will stay with him, if he chooses, for the rest of his life. They will be available to him when he needs them and when he wants them.

This is truly a gift.

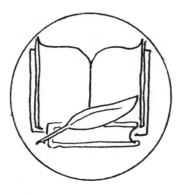

The Personal Journal

    Deep within each one of us is a well of information and experience that is not normally accessible. It is important to an individual's process of personal development and growth that this hidden information and experience become available. Writing in a personal journal is a powerful method for the individual to gain access to the inner resources and experiences that are a necessary part of self-discovery and growth. In this section we will discuss how to set up and use a personal journal and how this journal can be used effectively by the alcoholic client.

    The journal that I will be discussing is not a diary, nor is it just a record of what has happened and how we feel about our experiences. The personal journal, when used correctly, becomes an instrument that takes the writer on a journey into the inner landscape of his being. This journey is never really completed. The traveler resolves various conflicts in his life and discovers that as his life unfolds, he is constantly realizing new and more important insights.

    Two of the advantages of the journal process are that not only do insights occur, but the journal also provides an arena where past and present conflicts can be resolved.

    A person who is using a journal can explore as deeply into his life as he wishes; he can also move as fast or as slowly as he wishes. The journal is a self-paced and self-governing medium. The personal journal can become not only an integrated part of the counseling experience, but also a tool that the client can use on an ongoing basis.

The personal journal is ideal for the alcoholic client. In my experience as a counselor, I have found that many alcoholics find the medium of journal writing very comfortable. They seem to already have a feel for what the journal process is. I believe this is because most of the clients that I see have already completed written inventories about their lives and have discovered for themselves what a powerful tool writing can be.

The personal journal is not a substitute for the inventories that most alcoholics take in their A.A. recovery program. The journal, rather, continues that process.

There are many ways of keeping a journal, and there are many styles and structures that can be adopted. I feel that it is important to allow the journal to grow of its own accord. Each person's journal is a reflection of his own inner experiences and therefore is unique. The following are guidelines that I use when I am teaching a client how to set up a personal journal.

A fundamental aspect of the journal is that it is divided into sections, with dividers. Journal entries are made in the different sections of the journal. As the person grows, so does the journal. Every time we make a new section, we add a divider and write the heading of the section on the tab on the divider. This allows easy identification of the various journal sections.

It has been my experience that keeping the journal in a three-ring, looseleaf notebook is the most flexible and practical method. The personal journal is not a linear document, but an open-ended process. As our clients use the journal, they will be moving from one section to another and they will be adding material to different sections. A looseleaf notebook allows the journal to grow.

Every time an entry is made in the journal, it should be

dated. This is very important because it helps the writer position himself in the movement of his life. Without a sense of when something occurred, an individual can easily become confused, and this confusion can distort his memories. In many instances, it is advisable also to note the time of the day.

The following are the sections that I have found the most useful for the beginning journal writer. In the following examples I have used the journal entries of a former client of mine named Mary.

Daily Entries

This section is similar to a diary. Here we record the events of our lives as they happen, and record how we feel about these events. For Instance:

12/7/82

I talked to my ex-husband John today. I had the same old feelings of anger and frustration that I generally get when I talk to him.

It is important for the client to commit to making daily entries on a regular basis for at least a month. This helps the client get a feel for the journal and become accustomed to using it.

Personal History

Each of us has a personal history that is unique. It is this personal history that sets us apart from each other and from our closest family members. Even identical twins who were raised together have separate and distinct histories.

In this section of the journal, we record the events and experiences that make up our personal history. Much of the future work that will be done in the personal journal comes from the information in this section. It is here, in the personal history section, that we identify the experiences that have helped to shape and direct our lives.

The alcoholic client or the client from an alcoholic family has, in many instances, no sense of the continuity of his life. As a result of repressing painful emotional experiences, he has large chunks of time missing from his memory. He also has memories that are distorted because a situation is too painful to remember as it really happened, or the situation is remembered through an alcoholic haze. By using the personal history section, the client can re-establish a knowledge of, and a feeling for, his or her past.

Like the daily entries section, the personal history section is established by using a divider. The title on the tab of the divider is "Personal History."

To start this section, instruct the client to list ten or twelve of the major events of his or her life (remember to date the entry). These events, or milestones, are the markers that have helped to shape the client's life. It is important to keep this list of milestones to a manageable length; no more than a dozen events should be picked.

The following example is a list of Mary's milestones:

12/7/82

I was born.

I got sober.

I got married to John.

I went to college.

I did my 4th step inventory.

I was divorced.

I lost my job because of alcohol.

I moved to the Midwest.

I experienced God in my life.

My dad died of alcoholism.

I left the church.

I gave birth to my child.

It is not necessary that the list be in chronological order. What is important is that the client become aware of the events themselves, not their sequence.

When the list is complete, the client, at his or her leisure, will write about each of the milestones in detail. As he explores each event, he will gain a new sense of awareness, and new perspectives about his or her life. It is not necessary for the client to write at great length about these milestones; many times a page or even a paragraph will be enough to satisfy the client about that milestone period.

There will, however, be times when the client becomes aware that what he is writing about is causing emotional pain, that the issues he is examining are not resolved. When this happens the client can many times resolve these hidden issues by continuing to write about them in further detail, or by working through them with his counselor.

In the personal history section, I also suggest that the client make a list of the important persons in his life. This list can contain persons who are currently active in his or her life, or persons who are, for one reason or another, no longer a part of his day-to-day life.

Mary's list was:

Dad

Mom

Harry (my son)

John (my ex-husband)

Karen (my friend)

Tom (my brother)

Sandy (my sister)

Each of the important persons in the client's life should have his or her own section in the personal journal. In these sections the client can record how he feels about the relationship that he has with that person. I will continue to use Mary as an example.

Mary's ex-husband, John, was on her list of important people, and she also made entries in the daily entries section about him. It would be important, therefore, for Mary to have a section in her journal exclusively for John. In this section she would explore, in depth, her relationship with her ex-husband and resolve some of the conflict that continues to be a part of that relationship.

In order for the client, Mary, to work in her journal with her ex-husband in a meaningful way, she can use a technique called dialoguing. Dialoguing is the process of having a conversation, which is written down on paper, with another person, who is not present. During this conversation or dialogue, the person who is writing enters into a dialogue with the other person as if that person were present. As the dialogue progresses, the interaction between the two parties will become more and more spontaneous. As this process unfolds, the answers that the writer of the dialogue gets from the person with whom he is dialoguing can be very important in resolving issues that are blocking the growth of the relationship.

To break the ice in this conversation, Mary would first write a statement in the section about John, focusing on where their relationship is now. This focusing statement is short and to the point. Example:

12/8/82

Even though John and I have been divorced for almost two years, I still feel a lot of anger whenever I talk to him. But we have to talk; we see each other at A.A. meetings and we share custody of our son, Harry.

Next, Mary makes a list of the major events in John's life, the milestones that have shaped his life. They should be done in the first person, as if John were listing them himself. Example:

I was born on 11/2/39.

My father was an alcoholic.

My mother died when I was 13.

I left school to join the Navy.

I got married to Mary.

I had a son, Harry.

I got sober.

I was divorced.

I was remarried to June.

The purpose of the above list is to help Mary get a feel for how John's life has been. It is not necessary for Mary to make a new list each time she dialogues with John; she should, however, review the list of his milestones each time she dialogues with him and update it occasionally.

At this point, Mary would be ready to begin to dialogue with John. Dialoguing is a lot like writing a script for a play, except that one allows the dialogue to flow freely and spontaneously, not trying to control or edit it. Example:

Mary: Hello, John.
John: Hi.
Mary: I think that this is foolish.
John: That's O.K.
Mary: I get so mad at you.
John: I know you do, but you never tell me.
Mary: Well, I don't trust you. I think you might make fun of me.
John: You never used to give me the chance to talk to you. Your anger always got in the way.
Mary: I think I have a right to be angry.
John: Maybe you do, but it will always get in the way of our talking to each other if you can't tell me about it. I'm willing to listen.
Mary: Are you?
John: Yes, try me.

This script could go on, reaching deeper and deeper levels. It could also be done over and over until Mary resolves her hesitation about discussing her anger with John.

The journal is an ideal place for this type of conflict to be resolved. Dialoguing like this will, in many instances, bring about catharsis and release old negative emotions and negative programming.

To summarize: The journal should contain one section for each important person in your client's life, so that the client can gain insight and resolution in either positive or negative relationships. The dialoguing process is not just confined to people who are alive; it is often very valuable to dialogue with significant others who have died.

The Physical Body

Alcoholics, because of drinking and doing drugs, have generally lost contact with their physical selves. They have lost the ability to listen to what their bodies have to say to them. And yet each one of us has a wealth of wisdom contained in our physical body. We have huge amounts of information stored within us; all we need to do to gain access to this information is to ask.

The physical body section of the personal journal is the section where the client can re-establish this relationship with his physical self. In this section, the client will begin to communicate with his physical body, and this is done by dialoguing with the body.

To dialogue with the body, the same method is used as in the previous example, where Mary dialogued with her ex-husband, John. Have the client do the following:

1. Write a focusing statement about his relationship with his body.
2. List the events that have helped shape his body's life.
3. Dialogue with his body.

The following is an example of a dialogue that a client of mine, Eddie, had with his body.

Focusing Statement

12/3/79

I really feel out of touch with you, body. I have always felt that you were just something to endure. For many years I hated you and harmed you. Now I am trying to get to know you better and find out what your needs are.

Major life milestones

0 to 10 years old

Having tonsils out

Getting spanked

Not liking being tall and thin

Playing with my penis

10 to 20 years old

Masturbating

Not liking being tall

Not liking sports and geting hurt playing baseball

Sex with a woman

Drinking alcohol

20 to 30 years old

Being hurt in an accident

Being sick and having an operation

Taking drugs

Getting married

30 to 40 years old

Sick all the time from drugs and alcohol

Trying to kill myself

Stopping drinking and doing drugs

Stopping smoking

Starting to exercise, run and swim

Learning about my body
Dialoguing

Eddie: Hello, Body, are you there?

Body: Yes, I am.

Eddie: How are you doing?

Body: O.K.

Eddie: Are you still mad at me?

Body: Well, maybe a little bit. I don't think that you're taking as good care of me as you did a year ago.

Eddie: That's true, I guess.

Body: For sure. You have abused me almost all of our life. What you did to me with alcohol and drugs was terrible. The car wrecks, throwing up, all of that. Even shooting heroin. I never thought that you would do that.

Eddie: Now hold on. That's all in the past. I haven't used alcohol or drugs in four years.

Body: So you think that all you need to do is to stop drinking and all is fine.

Eddie: Yes, I do.

Body: Well, in case you didn't notice it, I still need care. How about some exercise and vitamins. How about eating right. Some of this garbage you feed me sucks.

Eddie: I know that I have fallen down, but I will try to get back on an exercise program and eat better. I know that I can, all I need to do is to just do it. Will you help me out?

Body: Sure, remember I have your own best interests at heart. Just take care of me and I will be around for a long time.

Eddie: O.K. I will try, and I will stay more in touch with you.

Dialoguing, as we can see in the above example, can bring surprising results. Most alcoholics have spent a lot of time and energy doing very unhealthy, hostile and almost lethal things to their bodies. My personal experience, and the experiences of my clients, confirm that it is vital to come to terms and to be at peace with the physical self. When this occurs, the body itself, through dialoguing, can use its wisdom to inform the self what to do to stay healthy.

I feel that the sections outlined above are important to the beginning journal writer. But this is just a start. The personal journal is not limited to the sections we have discussed. The client may add as many sections to the journal as he wishes. There is no limit to the size of the personal journal. Its size is governed by need and is limited only by the creativity of the writer.

Some of the other sections that I have found to be useful to my clients are:

Inner Guidance

Here the client has a place to begin to pursue and to understand the higher aspects of his nature, his spiritual self and intuition. He can dialogue with those people or spiritual masters from whom he would like to seek guidance. This valuable section can help the client to clarify his spiritual ideas and to formulate his own acceptable criteria for spiritual growth. Most of the clients that I have worked with find this to be a very important section.

Dreams

Have your clients record important dreams, for these can be the keys to what is going on in the unconscious mind. The client can also dialogue with his dreams. Dialoguing will help the client become clearer about what his dreams mean.

Meditation

Having a meditation section can be helpful to your client in several ways. Here he can record what type of meditation he is doing, how he feels about the meditation, whether anything important happens during the meditation. It is valuable to have a record of these feelings and experiences.

(Please see the chapter on Meditation for further information.)

Synthesis

The synthesis section is the place in the journal that provides space for the writer to tie up the loose ends of his life. Here he can record his insights and discoveries, the coming together of his ideas and intuitions. This can be the place for him to chronicle the spiritual awarenesses and experiences that he has had on his life journey.

The above are only a few of the sections that can be used in the personal journal. The journal will unfold and grow as your client grows. Encourage your client to experiment with his journal. It is important to stress that the journal need not be limited to just the written word. Many times our unconscious gives us messages in symbols or creative impulses. There could be a section for symbols and their interpretations, and a section for drawings, poetry, and other artwork as well.

Let the client's personal journal unfold and develop at its own rate. The journal will be unique to the client and it will take on a character of its own. It will speak to him.

This is the client's journal. This is an important point to remember. The client need not show any part of his journal to anyone, even his counselor. Stress to him that this is his private document, although he can share its content if he chooses.

I have found that when a client keeps a personal journal, the counseling session can become a richer and deeper experience. Clients are usually more than willing to share what they have written. Keeping a journal helps them feel that they are taking an active part in their own growth.

The journal is like a tapestry. When we weave the words of our lives in the journal, we create a beautiful work of art. Against the background of this artwork we dance and weave, discover and grow. Journal keeping is an art. Like any art, it must be practiced. The journal is also like a musical instrument and should be played. At some point in the process of journal writing, the journal writes itself, just as a musical instrument seems to play itself after the musician has become one with it.

The journal is a tool that can be used when necessary. The process of journal writing is a skill that your clients can use for the rest of their lives.

This is a gift.

---

*Dr. Ira Progoff has developed a journal called the Intensive Journal and has established a series of workshops that teach how to set up and use an Intensive Journal. He also has written "At a Journal Workshop" and "The Practice of Process Meditation." These books are musts for the serious student of the journal. I encourage you and your clients to read them and to attend one of the Intensive Journal Workshops.

Meditation

People have been using meditative techniques for thousands of years, and today millions of people meditate on a regular basis. In this section, we will explore some different ways of meditating and why meditating can be useful to the alcoholic client.

Most alcoholic clients I have worked with seem to have a lot of trouble turning off the constant internal dialogue that goes on inside their heads. In order to find serenity and emotional stability, it is necessary for the client to stop, or slow down, this internal dialogue. Meditation is a very effective way to halt or slow down this constant flow of thoughts.

The effects of meditation are four-fold. First, it assists the physical body with deep relaxation and the letting go of the physical manifestations of stress. Second, meditation helps to calm the emotional aspects of a person's nature. Third, meditation helps to give the meditator a clearer mental frame and the ability to focus more keenly. Fourth, meditation opens up a channel to the meditator's higher levels of consciousness and spiritual awareness.

These may seem to be rather extravagant claims, but they are not. As a counselor, one of the greatest gifts that you can give to your client is the gift of meditation.

It is important to remember that we cannot force a person to do anything that goes against his or her nature. Meditation cannot be forced on your clients. You can, however, offer it to them so they have the opportunity to choose whether or not they wish to try it.

Remember that some of your clients will not be able to meditate, and some of your clients will find that meditating seems to come naturally to them. All you can do is offer it.

There is a proper time in the counseling relationship for you to offer to teach your client how to meditate. It is important to have established a trusting relationship with your client already before you attempt to teach him or her to meditate.

A dialogue that might occur during a counseling session that could lead to a discussion about meditation might go something like this:

Client: It is sure hard for me to relax. It seems that every time I try to sit down and take it easy, all I do is think of things that I need to do.

Counselor: That sure can be a problem. What do you mean by thinking?

Client: I'm not sure, er, I guess I think a lot, I mean all the time. It's like having a recording in my head that never turns off.

Counselor: All of the time?

Client: Yes.

Counselor: Have you ever heard of meditation? A lot of people have used it to help quiet their minds.

Client: I've heard of it, but I'm not sure what it is.

Counselor: Would you like me to explain it to you?

Client: Yes, I'm interested in anything that would help me to stop thinking all of the time.

At this point, the counselor would explain to the client what meditation is and, very briefly, how to meditate.

I believe that it is important to keep the explanation of what meditation is and how to do it very simple. If the client chooses to start to meditate, then he will, on his own, begin to study meditation in more detail. All that we as counselors need to do is to introduce meditation to our clients, and, if they are interested, teach them the basic techniques. These basic techniques should be taught and demonstrated to the client during the counseling session.

Simply put, meditation is a process by which a person intentionally quiets his mind so he can become aware of his inner nature, his true self.

There are many ways to meditate. I am going to introduce you to two basic meditative methods, Breathing Meditation and Mantra Meditation.

Breathing Meditation

When we practice breathing meditation, all we do is become aware of the process of our breathing.

Have the client sit in a straight-backed chair, or in a cross-legged position on the floor. It is important that the person who is meditating be comfortable; it is hard to concentrate on breathing when you are in pain. Have your client close his eyes and ask him to pay attention to his breath as it flows in and out of his body. Tell him that he does not have to control his breath, but to breathe in a natural way.

Ask him to pay attention to the air as it enters his nose, to feel how cool it is. Ask him to feel how warm his outgoing breath is. Have him focus his attention on his breathing in a relaxed, noncontrolling manner. Tell him to be aware of the process of his breath as it flows in and out of his chest. Remind him, if thoughts come into his mind, to relax and let them go.

Have your client do this for about five to ten minutes. This is meditating on the breath. Easy, isn't it?

Meditating on a Sound

When you teach a client to meditate on a sound, you are using a technique called Mantra Meditation. In this type of meditation, instead of focusing the attention on breathing, we will teach the client to focus on a sound.

Many people have difficulty concentrating on breathing. They find it much easier to focus on a sound and repeat that sound over and over. As in breathing meditation, have your client sit either cross-legged on the floor or in a straight-backed chair. Either position is O.K. The important thing is to be comfortable.

When using mantra meditation, it is important to pick a sound that has very little or no meaning to the client. A sound that is used many times in this type of meditation is the word "one," which is repeated over and over. The sound that I like to teach my clients is "So-Hum." It does not mean anything to the client and it has a pleasant rhythm. The sound of "OM" is also very widely used for mantra meditation. Any of the above sounds is fine to use.

Have the client sit and say the sound softly, over and over, saying it softer and softer each time he says it until he is no longer saying the sound out loud, but is repeating it silently inside of his head. Have him do this for five to ten minutes. Remind him that when thoughts come to him, all he need do is to gently return to the sound. When the client wishes to meditate at home, all he needs to do is to find a quiet place to sit, focus on the sound, and say it silently over and over to himself.

It is very important to inform your client that it is natural for him to forget that he is meditating and to start to think about other things. When this occurs, just tell him to refocus on the breath or the sound and gently return to meditating.

Many people get frustrated and angry because they cannot concentrate and their minds wander. This is very natural and happens to almost everyone. The meditative process will be effective even if most of the time meditating is spent in wandering thoughts. For the beginning meditator, the most important aspects of meditation are the willingness to sit and meditate, and to continue to return to the meditative state when the thoughts wander.

I suggest that my clients meditate the first thing in the morning, before they drink coffee or smoke. I believe that this helps to start the day with an attitude of serenity. Meditating in the morning, before coffee or cigarettes, also interrupts the addictive cycle of these two drugs. This enhances the possibility of the client's letting go of these addictions.

If, however, it is difficult for the client to meditate in the morning, select a more convenient time. Although I prefer the morning, anytime during the day will do.

It is very important to agree upon a length of time that your client will meditate. The generally-accepted length of time for meditation is twenty minutes once or twice a day. My experience has been that many newly-sober people (under a year) have a great deal of difficulty sitting still for that length of time, so it should be presented not as an absolute, but as something to shoot for.

On the other hand, some clients will wish to sit in meditation for hours at a time. This extreme should also be avoided. Many alcoholics have a tendency to overdo things. Then they get burned out on them.

I like to have my clients start off meditating for five to ten minutes once a day. If they do this on a regular basis, then they will naturally increase the length of time that they meditate. They will grow in meditation at their own rates.

When a person begins to meditate and quiets the internal dialogue, many things happen. When the mind becomes quiet, the meditator makes room for many repressed emotions and experiences to bubble to the surface. When these repressed feelings surface, then the meditator can let go of them.

Picture the mind as a lake, whose surface is full of ripples caused by the wind of our thoughts. When we meditate, that wind is slowed down and stopped. When this happens, we are allowed a glimpse into the depths of our very being. When we look into these depths, we are free to let go of many old negative emotions and thoughts. This is truly a gift.

Affirmations

We are what we think. There is a great deal of power in the thoughts, spoken words, and written statements that we make about ourselves. A direct correlation exists between the way a person thinks about himself and how he behaves. It is difficult for many of us to imagine how much of our own reality we create by how we think and speak.

Current research does, however, indicate that to a large extent, we create our own realities with our thoughts. Research in the health sciences definitely proves that thoughts and attitudes contribute to the healing process, and that these same thoughts and attitudes also contribute to ill health. The difference is whether these thoughts are positive or negative.

Alcoholism is a disease of the body, emotions, mind and spirit. There are very few other diseases that succeed in isolating a person from loved ones, and from the human community, like alcoholism does. As a person becomes more and more a slave to alcoholism, he becomes more and more withdrawn, and the way he thinks about himself becomes increasingly negative. These negative thoughts are also reinforced by the way the alcoholic's family and the rest of the world treat him.

An alcoholic does not know who he is. His self-image is very poor, his thoughts about others are negative, and the way he speaks about himself is negative.

In recovery, after the alcoholic is not drinking, these negative thoughts and feelings continue to plague him and can continue to do so for a long time. There are many recovered alcoholics who have stopped drinking, but still have the same old negative thinking and feeling patterns. A vital part of the recovery process is the reconstruction and integration of positive thoughts and the rebuilding of positive self-image.

We as counselors can give our clients a tool that is extremely effective in assisting in this positive process. This powerful tool is the creative use of affirmations.

Affirmations are positive thoughts that a person deliberately introduces into his or her consciousness, so that the old, negative programming is replaced by new and positive thoughts.

The alcoholic's negative programming runs deep and comes from two basic sources. The first is compulsive drinking itself. The irrational and insane behavior caused by compulsive drinking produces feelings of shame and guilt in the alcoholic. These feelings of shame and guilt are not experienced directly but are often translated into negative feelings of self-worth and self-image that the alcoholic keeps in his unconscious mind.

Secondly, negative programming also comes from the way the alcoholic learned to view himself when he was a child. As a child, the alcoholic, like all children, received both verbal and nonverbal messages from the important adults in his life. Many times these messages were translated into negative programming. As adults, this negative programming is still carried around in the unconscious mind.

A person who is in the process of recovery from alcoholism and who has this negative programming is constantly in a state of internal conflict. He feels good about himself for not drinking, but he still has this old unconscious programming telling him that he is a "bad person."

Affirmations can, over a period of time, replace those old negative programs. It is vital to remember that affirmations are not used to repress feelings. They are not used to stuff emotions. Alcoholics have a great deal of experience with how to stuff feelings and emotions; we don't need to give them another technique. The process of releasing stuffed negative emotions must occur for the alcoholic to grow. Affirmations create a new and fresh point of view, rather than just replace the old ideas.

There are a number of different ways to do affirmations. They ways that I have found to be the most effective are:

1. Spoken silently to oneself.

2. Said out loud.

3. Spoken out loud to another person.

4. Spoken into a recorder and played back.

5. Written down on paper.

The following statements are guidelines that are helpful when teaching clients to use affirmations:

1. Affirmations are positive statements. We teach people to affirm the positive rather than reinforce the negative.

2. Affirmations are most effective when they are short and to the point. Keep them simple.

3. Affirmations are kept in the present.

4. Affirmations affirm what one desires rather than what one wants to get rid of.

5. Affirmations take time to get results. They should not be put on a timetable; the results will unfold at their own speed.

6. Affirmations are repeated each day. It is the repetition of the positive affirmation that produces the desired result.

Some time ago, I had a client named Helen. Helen was married to an alcoholic. Her husband had been sober for four years but had returned to drinking, and had been drinking for about two years when Helen came to me for counseling.

Like many people who are married to alcoholics, Helen had an extremely low self-image. She could not imagine what she could do to change her current living situation, but she knew that she had to do something because she was in a lot of emotional pain. Like many women in her situation, she also blamed herself for her husband's drinking problems.

After Helen and I had been in two counseling sessions, we worked out a simple affirmation that she could do at home and at work. The affirmation was, "I, Helen, love myself."

Helen's instructions were to say this affirmation ten times to herself every morning.

"I, Helen, love myself."

"I, Helen, love myself."

"I, Helen, love myself."

"I, Helen, love myself."

"I, Helen, love myself."

"I, Helen, love myself."

"I, Helen, love myself."

"I, Helen, love myself."

"I, Helen, love myself."

"I, Helen, love myself."

Helen's self-image was so poor that at first she was unable to say the affirmation out loud. After a number of weeks she could say the affirmation out loud to herself, at which point I had her say the affirmation out loud to herself each morning while looking in her bedroom mirror.

It was a major turning point in Helen's life when, during a counseling session, she was able to look me in the eyes and tell me, "I, Helen, love myself."

Each client is different, and affirmations should be tailored to the individual needs of each client. In Helen's case we needed to start very gently, with her saying the affirmation first silently to herself, then out loud to the mirror, and finally out loud to me.

Over the months that Helen and I were in the counseling relationship, she continued to do her affirmation and her feelings of self-love got stronger and stronger. The result of this work was that Helen finally left the unhealthy relationship and rebuilt her life. I received a telephone call from her a year after she moved out of town and she was doing fine. And still doing her affirmation.

I have gotten some very positive feedback from clients who have used their affirmations in creative ways. A powerful method for using affirmations is to have the client record the affirmation onto a tape and play the tape back at convenient times such as on the car stereo while driving to and from work, or playing the tape when doing housework. As the tape is being played back, the client can either just listen to the tape, or say the affirmation along with the recording.

The most powerful way to use affirmations is to write them down on paper. This method strongly reinforces the affirmation, because as the affirmation is being written, it is seen, said to one's self, and "felt" as the act of writing it is taking place.

Do not overload the client with affirmations. Giving the client four or five affirmations to work with can be very time consuming and discouraging. One or two affirmations at a time is best. Remember: You are teaching the client not only how to use affirmations, but also how to create them.

Changes in attitude and point of view occur very rapidly with clients who use written affirmations. Written affirmations are most effective when written ten to twenty times each day. I am partial to morning, but anytime during the day is effective. (I choose morning because if I don't do things in the morning, I have a tendency not to ever get around to them.)

To be most powerful, the written affirmation is done in the first person (I), the second person (you), and the third person (he or she). Here is an example involving a former client of mine named Steven. Like many chemically-dependent people, Steven was having a difficult time getting in touch with his emotions. He felt very "stuck." He knew that he was blocking emotions, but he did not know how to get "unstuck."

The affirmation that we worked out for Steven was:

"I, Steven, am capable and willing to experience all of my emotions."

This part of the affirmation is written in the first person and makes the statement that even with old negative ideas about being unable to express emotions, he, Steven, is affirming that today he can express emotions. (Remember that to be effective, affirmations are done in the present tense.)

"You, Steven, are capable and willing to experience all of your emotions."

This part of the affirmation is written in the second person and makes the statement that although Steven was once taught that showing emotions was unacceptable behavior, today he is allowed to show emotion.

"He, Steven, is capable and willing to express all of his emotions."

This part of the affirmation is written in the third person and makes the statement that regardless of the role models that Steven had, and regardless of what people said about him, Steven is capable and willing to express his emotions today.

The whole affirmation would be:

"I, Steven, am capable and willing to experience all of my emotions."

"You, Steven, are capable and willing to experience all of your emotions."

"He, Steven, is capable and willing to experience all of his emotions."

An important point to remember is that when strong positive affirmations are used, they will, in most cases, bring up strong negative feelings from the person's subconscious. When a person who has had strong negative programming uses a positive affirmation, the negative feelings that are a part of that old programming will surface. This is particularly true when the affirmation is being written.

When a client is writing an affirmation, it is important to acknowledge these negative feelings. This acknowledgment is an integrated part of the process of letting go of the old programming. During the process of writing the affirmation, the client must also write down the negative feelings that he experiences. I have found that jotting down the negative thoughts after writing the affirmation is the most effective method for noting the negative response.

After the client has written the affirmations, he can review the negative responses. These will give him insights into the unconscious negative programming that is standing in the way of the fulfillment of his affirmation. After the client has written the negative responses for approximately four days, he will have a good idea of what is standing in the way of the affirmation. At this point the client would discontinue writing the negative responses and just write the affirmation.

The negative responses that surface during writing the affirmations make excellent material for discussion during counseling sessions.

Many times, as the client writes his affirmation, he will move from negative responses to more positive responses.

During this process of moving from the negative to the positive, the client may even find himself writing encouraging statements about the affirmation.

Continuing to use Steven as an example, the affirmation and his responses were as follows:

"I, Steven, am capable and willing to experience all of my emotions." (No, I can't do that.)

"You, Steven, are capable and willing to experience all of your emotions." (I was told that it was bad to show emotions.)

"He, Steven, is capable and willing to express all of his emotions." (No, I'm not.)

"I, Steven, am capable and willing to experience all of my emotions." (What if someone sees me cry?)

"You, Steven, are capable and willing to experience all of your emotions." (I'm afraid to let people in.)

"He, Steven, is capable and willing to express all of his emotions." (I feel so sad.)

"I, Steven, am capable and willing to experience all of my emotions." (Dad never cried.)

"You, Steven, are capable and willing to experience all of your emotions." (This makes me feel sick.)

"He, Steven, is capable and willing to express all of his emotions." (I won't be a man if I feel.)

"I, Steven, am capable and willing to experience all of my emotions." (I'm afraid of what's bottled up inside me.)

"You, Steven, are capable and willing to experience all of your emotions." (I'll lose control.)

"He, Steven, is capable and willing to express all of his emotions." (The last time I cried I was ten.)

"I, Steven, am capable and willing to experience all of my emotions." (Maybe I can.)

"You, Steven, are capable and willing to experience all of your emotions." (It might not be so bad.)

"He, Steven, is capable and willing to express all of his emotions." (I think I will be able to.)

As can be seen in the above example, while Steven was writing his affirmation, he moved from the negative responses that he wrote in the beginning, to more positive and encouraging responses.

Change can happen quickly when affirmations are used. Not only can affirmations be used to root out the old negative programming that alcoholics have, but they can also be used to deal with immediate situations that cause fearful responses.

One client called me on the phone and told me that she wanted to call a man that she was interested in to ask him to a party, but she was afraid to make the call. She had to make the call that night because the party was the next day. I asked her what kind of affirmation would fit this situation, and she created this affirmation:

"I, Kim, can ask Joe for a date."

She wrote this several times and then made the telephone call.

Many alcoholics have difficulties in relationships. The isolation that is brought about by drinking does not lend itself either to attracting a healthy mate, or to being a healthy partner in a relationship. Some excellent affirmations to use with clients in difficult relationships are:

"I, _____, am a healthy person, and I am capable of having a loving, intimate relationship.

I, _____, no longer need _____ to make me feel good about myself.

I love myself and I deserve a good relationship.

Affirmations are not really very new. People have been using them for years, even in the addictions field. How many times have you heard, "I, _____, am clean and sober today."? Now that's a powerful affirmation.

Most of my clients really enjoy doing affirmations. It gives them an extremely positive payoff for doing a small amount of work, and helps them feel good about themselves. Affirmations give the client an opportunity to take a visible, active part in his growth.

The following is a list of some of the affirmations that I use with my clients on a regular basis:

"Every day in every way I am getting better, better, and better."

I accept all of my feelings as a part of myself.

The more I love myself, the more I am capable of loving.

I am a whole, healthy human being.

My life is unfolding as it should.

I, _____, am lovable.

I, _____, am loving.

I, _____, deserve love.

My true self is my sober self.

My life has meaning and purpose.

I am living my life one day at a time.

Today I can stay sober and happy.

Many of my clients have a spiritual unrest within them,

and almost to a person, they have a desire to grow in a spiritual direction. I encourage them in their personal spiritual quests, for I have found that it is this inward searching and the spiritual way of life that gives the lives of many recovered people a sense of meaning and purpose.

Affirmations used in a spiritual context are powerful. I have found that clients who seek to expand and grow spiritually use this type of affirmation with great enthusiasm and effectiveness. Below are some examples of affirmations that have a spiritual dimension and direction.

My higher self is guiding me in everything I do.

The Christ within me is creating miracles in my life today.

I am letting go and letting God.

I, _____, am living in the presence of divine love and light.

I, _____, am at one with the spirit of the universe.

If the client is using a personal journal, it is useful to have him or her create a section for written affirmations. He will then be able to track his use of affirmations over a period of time. This will demonstrate, first-hand, what a powerful tool affirmations are.

Your clients have the wisdom to know what affirmations will work for them. After they have been using affirmations for a while, they will, in many cases, change the affirmations that were originally given to them. This is a wonderful step; encourage it. Teach your clients to create their own affirmations. This will be a gift that they will be able to use for the rest of their lives.

Creative Visualization

It is the nature of the human being to think and to imagine. We are what we think and are capable of becoming what we imagine. There is a power in our imagination that is, as yet, not completely understood. We do know that the ability to use creative imagination is open to everyone. All humans have the ability to imagine and to dream.

The process of creative visualization is the conscious directing of the imagination to produce a desired result. The human mind is a powerful resource, and its ability and potential are, to a large extent, unknown. We do know, however, that using the imagination in a controlled and directed manner can produce results in healing the physical body, stabilizing the emotions, quieting the mind, and communicating with the inner spirit.

Each one of us has the ability to use inner vision. This inner vision is, however, not the same for each individual. Most of the clients that I have worked with have had the ability to "see pictures" in their mind's eye. There is, however, a sizeable number of people who get turned off to visualization because they cannot "see" these pictures. These people "see" in a different way; their inner experience is more a feeling rather than a seeing. Others "think about" what they want to visualize; they don't see pictures or feel. Some do all of the above, or at any given time, do one or the other.

The important point is, we as human beings have the ability to have inner visions, and have the capability to imagine. People do this in different ways; the results are the same.

Creative visualization is a powerful tool that you, as a counselor, can give to your client. It is important to remember that what we dream to be, we can become, and what we imagine can come to pass.

Thoughts are energy. They have power. When the powerful energy of thoughts is directed and focused, the results can be amazing. Most people take their thoughts for granted. They believe that, since they have a seemingly endless and constant stream of thoughts flowing through their minds, these thoughts are unimportant and carry no power. But thoughts are powerful, even random or trivial ones, and they always transmit a powerful message to our subconscious.

The alcoholic client has been caught up in negative thoughts and behaviors. Long after the drinking has stopped, these negative patterns can and do cause emotional pain and physical ill health. Through the use of creative visualization, you can help your client to move away from his old, negative thinking patterns.

Thoughts and imagination have energy and power. When we direct our thoughts and imagination in a positive direction, a positive result is produced. Conversely, if thoughts and imagination are directed in a negative direction, then we can expect negative outcomes. Fear attracts more fear and anger produces nothing but anger. The following story is an example of negative imagination in action.

A man was driving along a deserted country road. It was late in the evening and very dark. Suddenly there was a loud sound, like a gunshot; the man pulled to the side of the road, got out of the car, and discovered that he had a flat tire. When he opened his trunk, he found that he had left his tire jack at home.

Off in the distance the man could see a light in a farmhouse window. Not wanting to spend the night in the car, he decided that he would walk to the farm and ask the farmer if he would lend him a tire jack.

As he started to walk along the road to the farmhouse, the man began to imagine what would happen when he talked to the farmer. His thoughts went something like this:

It's late and the farmer is most likely asleep. When I ring his doorbell, I'll wake him up and he'll probably be angry.

Farmers don't generally like city people like me anyway.

He will probably tell me to get off of his property.

He might even have a gun and run me off, or turn his dogs loose on me.

Farmers are all a bunch of ill-tempered jerks anyway.

They love to give strangers like me a hard time.

By the time the man reached the farmhouse, he had become angry and defensive. When he rang the doorbell and the farmer opened the door, the man shouted angrily at the farmer, "You can stick your jack where the sun doesn't shine, I wouldn't take it if you offered it to me!" The man then turned and stalked away from the amazed and confused farmer.

This may seem like a far-fetched story, but time and again I have seen my clients imagine themselves into situations that are not any less absurd than the above.

On the other hand, I have also seen clients let go of old negative thoughts through the use of creative visualization. The mind can be trained, and it can be controlled. Thoughts can be redirected, and the negative imaginings that have become a part of the alcoholic's thoughts can become positive visualizations. The process is simple.

The basic steps to the process of creative visualization are:

1. Have a clear and specific idea or picture of the desired objective or goal.

2. Set the desired objective or goal in the mind.

3. Focus on the objective or goal often.

4. Give is positive energy (good thoughts).

When you are working with an alcoholic client who has had years of practice using visualization and imagination in negative ways, it is important that you proceed slowly and simply. Doing easy and simple visualizations will quickly give the client a history of successes, and will give him the confidence that creative visualization will work for him.

The first step in introducing a client to the use of creative visualization is to help him realize that he can use his imagination in a healthy and constructive way.

A former client of mine, Ken, was fearful of using his imagination. For years, he had always thought in negative terms, and when any situation came up, all he could see was a negative outcome. Thus, most of his important life situations resulted in negative outcomes. Ken did not want to use his mind and inner vision; he did not trust them.

In order for Ken to gain the experience of having positive results using his imagination, I took him step-by-step through a relaxation exercise using creative visualization. I have found that this step-by-step procedure works extremely well with clients like Ken who have had a lot of negative experiences using their imaginations.

To begin this creative visualization relaxation exercise, I had Ken lay down, become quiet, close his eyes and listen to the sound of my voice.

(. . . indicates a pause of approximately 10 to 15 seconds.)

Relax . . .Breathe normally and without straining or trying to control . . . Continue to concentrate on your breath . . . Allow yourself to breathe easily and slowly . . . (Allow one to two minutes to let the client be still and concentrate on breathing) . . . Continue to breathe, slowly and quietly . . . Allow your mind to scan your body . . . Find any areas in your body where you experience tension or strain. When you find an area that is tense, direct your thoughts to that area of your body, and with every out breath imagine that you are releasing and letting go of the tension and strain . . . (Allow the client one to two minutes to experience letting go of the tension, occasionally reminding him to breathe and to relax) . . . Relax and continue to breathe . . . Now I want you to imagine that you are in a place where you can be totally relaxed, a place where you can be completely comfortable and at ease, without disturbances or interruptions . . . This place of deep relaxation could be a sunlit meadow, or a hot bath. It can be any place that you choose to be . . . (Allow the client a minute or two to find his place of relaxation) . . . Nod your head when you have this place of deep relaxation . . . (When the client nods his head, continue) . . . Continue to stay in your place of deep relaxation . . .

If other thoughts interrupt you, or your mind wanders to another subject, gently remind yourself to return to your place of relaxation . . . (Let the client stay in this place of relaxation for three or four minutes) . . . You are now getting ready to become more and more aware of the outside world . . . Remember that you can return to this place of deep relaxation anytime that you wish, just by breathing slowly and remembering your special place of relaxation . . . Become aware of your body . . . Feel the weight of your clothes against your skin . . . Become aware of your breath . . . When you are ready, open your eyes.

When the relaxation exercise is completed, discuss it with your client. Talk about where his place of relaxation was. This processing will help to reinforce the exercise.

Ken had a place of relaxation that was on the shore of a quiet blue lake. He pictured himself sitting on the shore of this lake during a summer afternoon, with the warm summer sun shining down on him. Ken found that when he began to tense up, or when he wanted to relax at night after work, all he had to do was to imagine himself back at his quiet blue lake. Then he became more relaxed.

After your client has done this relaxation visualization several times with you, and at home, he will begin to notice that by using the power of his imagination, he will be able to relax when he is feeling tense and uptight. This is an important step. Once your client has a record of success with using creative visualizations, he can then move on to more complex visualizations.

When you are leading a client in a creative visualization, it is very important to inform the client that you are just guiding him. Remind him that you are not in control of him, and that at any time during the visualization he has the power and ability to open his eyes and stop the process. I had one client who, when she closed her eyes and tried to visualize, became filled with dread and fear. Before we could do any work with the creative visualization process, it was necessary to work through her fear of closing her eyes and trying to imagine.

It is very important to allow your client to proceed at his or her own pace. Once the process of using visualization begins, the client will proceed at his or her own rate.

All of the alcoholic clients that I have worked with have suffered, at one level or another, from anger and resentment. Using creative visualization to assist a client to release this anger and resentment is extremely effective. Many clients simply don't know how to begin to let go of it.

Accepting that the anger is there is the first step in the process of letting go of it. Unfortunately, many people get stuck in the acceptance step and keep experiencing their anger, rage, and resentment over and over. They have done all that they know to do to let go of these feelings; they have talked about it, written about it, found out where it comes from, talked (if possible) to the other person about their anger, and still they have not been able to release it.

Kay, a former client of mine. is an excellent example of how to use creative visualization to let go of anger. Kay had been involved in a relationship, and when it ended, she still felt a lot of anger and resentment toward her ex-boyfriend. Kay had done all that she knew to let go of her anger; she had written about it, discussed it, even confronted her ex-boyfriend with it. Although Kay felt that these actions had produced relief, she still felt that she was holding on to anger; she really wanted to let go, but she did not know how.

After Kay and I had discussed her anger, we decided that doing a creative visualization might help her to let go of it.

I asked Kay to find a comfortable position, to close her eyes and listen to the sound of my voice. I told her that she was in control and could open her eyes any time she wished. Then I guided Kay through the following creative visualization (. . . indicates a pause of 10 to 15 seconds):

Relax and listen to the sound of your breath . . . Pay attention to how it feels to breathe . . .Relax and go inward . . . Continue to breathe; with every outgoing breath, feel yourself becoming more and more relaxed . . . Scan your body; if you find any areas of tension or discomfort, with every outgoing breath let go of the tension . . . Nod you head to let me know when you are totally relaxed and at ease . . . (Here I waited for Kay to nod; the process took approximately three minutes) . . .

Picture the man that you have the resentment against . . . Picture him in great detail; see the color of his hair, notice what color his eyes are, be aware of what he is wearing . . . When you have a clear picture of this man, let me know by nodding your head . . . (Kay nods her head) . . . Now I want you to surround this man with a golden light . . . Hold him in this light . . . Think thoughts of forgiveness and love towards this man . . . Keeping him in the golden light, say to him, "I, Kay, forgive you" . . . Say this several times to yourself . . . Now become aware of the outer world . . . Pay attention to your breathing . . . When you feel ready, open your eyes.

I asked Kay to do this visualization once in the morning and once in the evening. At first she felt little relief from her resentment and anger, but after a week of doing this visualization, she began to have kinder feelings towards this man, and after just a few weeks she had no resentment.

This technique does work, and it works fast. I have had clients get rid of their anger and resentments after only a few sessions of using creative visualization. Sometimes, when the anger is extremely deep-seated, the process may take more time. But if the client is willing to do the visualization, the anger and resentment will leave.

Once again, it is important to remember that the creative visualization process is not used to repress emotions. If the person is not ready, or willing, to let go of the anger (or any other negative emotion), he will experience that emotion more intensely when he attempts to use creative visualization. This is an ideal time to assist him or her in processing this emotion.

Creative visualization can be used to achieve many different goals. It is particularly effective for alcoholics to get in contact with their higher natures, or higher selves.

The higher self is that part of the human consciousness which represents the highest aspirations of the human spirit. It is that aspect of human nature from which love, beauty, unity and the desire to grow toward a higher ideal radiate. It is from the higher self that inspiration and intuitive awareness spring. The higher self is the well of the soul; it has a connection to universal truth and wisdom that defies logic.

The higher self can be effectively contacted by using creative visualization. I have never had an alcoholic client who did not wish to find out more about his or her spiritual nature. It is through contact and dialogue with the higher self that the alcoholic client can achieve and maintain a rapport and relationship with his spiritual self. In many instances, it is this relationship that gives the alcoholic a sense of purpose that he has been yearning for to feel complete.

The visualization that I have found to be most successful in guiding my clients to the awareness of their higher selves follows (. . . indicates a pause of 10 to 15 seconds):

Find a comfortable position, either sitting or lying down on your back. Relax . . . Pay attention to your breathing . . . Feel your breath going in and out of your nose . . . Feel the coolness of the air as it enters your nose . . . Relax . . . Continue to breathe in an uncontrolled and relaxed manner . . . Allow your breath to come freely . . . (Pause and allow 2 to 3 minutes to pass) . . . When you are relaxed, scan your body for any points or areas of tension or pain . . . If you find an area of stress, breathe into it and allow the tension and the pain to flow away with your outgoing breath . . .

Imagine yourself standing on a path in a large woods . . . It is a woods full of large trees . . The trees are full of leaves . . . The sunlight filters down through the trees and gives the forest a twilight feeling . . . You begin to walk along the path . . . As you walk along this path, you see how beautiful the forest is . . . Ahead of you there is a clearing . . . a clearing at the end of the path . . . As you walk toward the clearing, you realize that it is a meadow . . . You step out of the forest into

the meadow . . . It is very pretty . . . There are
flowers and butterflies . . . You slowly follow the
path across the meadow . . . At the end of the
path on the other side of the meadow is a tall
mountain . . .

As you walk toward the mountain, you see that
there is a white stone stairway that leads up the
side of the mountain . . . You cannot see the top
of the mountain, but you begin the climb the stairs
. . . As you climb, you realize that you are feeling
lighter and freer, as if you had left all of your cares
and troubles below . . . You continue to climb and
you continue to feel better and better . . .

When you reach the top of the white stairway, you
see a large, white stone building . . . It is very
beautiful . . . You walk to the steps leading into
this building and climb them . . . At the top of the
steps is a large door . . . You open the door and
enter the building . . . The room that you step
into is large and beautifully furnished . . . It has
rich wall hangings and is filled with the type of
furnishings that you like . . . You stand in the
room for a moment and take in the beauty of
it . . .

At the far end of the room you see a door . . . You
slowly walk across the room to the door . . . As
you approach this door, you feel at peace and
relaxed . . . You know that on the other side of
the door you will meet a being who is full of
wisdom and love . . . You reach out and open the
door and step into a room . . . The room is simply
furnished . . . But it is beautiful . . . As you stand
there in this room you became aware of another
presence in the room with you . . . This presence
radiates love and wisdom . . . You have no fear or
doubts . . . You stand there and bask in the love
of this being . . . if you have any questions that
you feel that you need or want to ask this being, ask
them now . . . (Pause for 2 or 3 minutes to allow
your client to ask any questions that he may have)...
As you say farewell to this being, you have the knowledge that you may return to this place any time you
wish . . .

You leave the small room and enter the large hall ...
You walk slowly through the hall to the door and go
out to the steps . . . You go down the steps and
walk to the stairway leading down the mountain ...
When you reach the stairway you turn and look
back at the large white building . . . You know
that you can return there whenever you wish . . .
You turn and go down the stairway . . . When
you reach the bottom of the stairway, you walk
along the path, across the meadow . . . You
continue across the meadow on the path and
enter the forest . . . You feel fine and at peace
with yourself . . . As you walk along the path
through the forest, you reflect on the events that
have just happened . . . You feel fine . . . As you
continue to walk along the forest path, you begin
to fell that you are back in your body . . . You pay
attention to your breath as you breathe in and
out . . . When you are ready, open your eyes.

The above visualization generally takes about twenty
minutes. It is important that enough time is left at the end
of the visualization for your client to process his experiences.
Most times, after this type of visualization, your client will
feel a need to share what has occurred. This opening up to
the higher self of the client is an important step in his growth
process. Treat it with respect.

I have used this visualization with many clients; it is
powerful. Many times this experience is the beginning of the
client's opening up to his or her own inner wisdom, realizing
his or her own spiritual nature.

Creative visualization is a gift that you can give to your
client that will help him open up to the power of his creative
imagination. With this gift he can let go of old negative
thoughts and refocus his mind on a more positive idea of life
and his relation to it. The power of the imagination is
unlimited; the mind, when used in a positive way, can open
up ways of being that were never even considered. The
recovered alcoholic need not continue to be afraid of his
mind and his imagination. He can learn to use them in
powerful and creative ways. His imagination can become his
ally and friend.

With creative visualization all things become possible. It can open doorways to the imagination and the creative self. But these things are dwarfed by the potential for growth of the spirit. Becoming aware of the dimensions of the spirit, and finding a way to get in touch with, and have access to, the higher self is possible with the use of creative visualization. This is truly a gift.

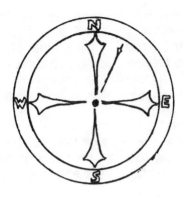

Positioning

During the ongoing process of our daily lives, we have a periodic need to assess who we are and where we are going. Many of us feel overwhelmed by the day-to-day activities that make up our lives, and it is important to find a way to stop and look at the specific actions that we take, as well as listen to the specific thoughts that we have about ourselves.

Positioning is a way to do this—to stop our individual process and take a look at what we are really doing in our lives. Without positioning we tend to become unaware of the subtle changes of direction that our thinking takes; we could begin to act in a way that is inconsistent with the way that we think we are acting.

Many of the alcoholic clients that I work with are unable to position themselves in the ongoing process of their lives, and it's easy to see why. Through all the years of drinking and drugging, they have been unable to reconcile their behavior with their values. This is part of the disease of addiction. The addict does not act in a manner that is consistent with his value system. So it is no wonder recovered alcoholics have trouble taking stock of themselves; either they have no previous experience at it, and so do not know where to begin, or else they are horrified by what they find when they take a sober look at the past.

One of the most common complaints that I hear from

clients is that they feel overwhelmed by their lives. Things seem out of control. They feel that they are on a roller coaster and that everything in life is just a blur. When I meet with clients who feel like this, I try to assist them to find out what is actually happening in their lives, and what their position is in the ongoing process of their lives.

Jan, a former client of mine, first started counseling with the complaint that she felt overwhelmed by life, that things were moving along too fast for her; she never seemed to have time to do the things she enjoyed.

After we had talked for a while, I asked her to tell me three things that she liked to do, that gave her a great deal of pleasure.

Her responses were:

I like to go camping.

I like to go to the movies.

I enjoy reading novels.

Jan was very clear on what she liked to do. I asked her to write these things down on a piece of paper. Then I asked her to put the date when she had last done each of these activities. When we compared what she stated she liked to do with the last date she had actually done it, she was amazed.

She had not gone camping for over two years. She was not sure when she had been to the movies last, but it had been more than several months ago. She had been reading the same novel for over six months, never seeming to have time to finish it.

When Jan and I first discussed the things she did for pleasure, she talked about the above activities as if these were things she did on a regular basis, but her thinking and her actions clearly did not match up. In her mind she "thought" she was doing fun things but, in reality, she wasn't. She had gotten so caught up in the movement of her life and the fast pace of her day-to-day existence that she had forgotten to have fun.

This is easy to do. Many of my clients forget to have fun; so do counselors. We forget to do the things that give us pleasure. We don't realize what we are doing on a daily basis; we draw from the memory of having had pleasure in the past and then wonder why the present seems so unfulfilling.

When beginning a positioning session, it is important to ask specific questions. That's why I ask a client to write out what he likes, and write out the date when he last did the activity. The writing brings the activity into focus; the client stops the process of his life for a moment and looks directly at what he is doing in light of what he thinks he is doing.

When Jan compared her list and the corresponding dates, she easily realized why she was feeling overwhelmed. She and I made a contract that during the next week she would take time to do at least one of the things on her fun list. Over a period of time Jan reincorporated the fun activities into her life. The feeling of being swept along by life and of being out of control left her. Her life became much more balanced.

Another important aspect of using the fun list is that in some instances, parts of the list will prove to be invalid; a client may think that he enjoys a particular activity, but when he actually does the activity, he finds that he no longer enjoys doing it.

I asked Joe, a man who came to me because he felt that his life was dull and uninteresting, to make a fun list. His list was:

I like to hunt.

I like to fish.

I like boating.

Joe had become caught up in the same trap as Jan; he had allowed his life to become so busy that he did not do anything for fun. We made a contract that he would begin to reintegrate fun activities into his life. After several experiences with hunting, Joe found out that he really did not enjoy hunting. The only reason he had gone hunting in the past was to get away from his family and drink. With this discovery, Joe was able to let go of the idea that he liked to hunt; he stopped wasting energy thinking about an activity that he really did not enjoy. He could then explore new ways to have fun and integrate them into his life.

A majority of alcoholics who come from alcoholic families simply don't know how to have fun. They never learned how, and as sober adults, they really have no idea how to go about enjoying themselves. The concept of playing or having fun is, for the most part, missing in an alcoholic household, and children in such an environment rarely learn how to set aside time for fun activities. When they grow up and leave the alcoholic family, they have a good chance of either becoming caught up in their own addiction, or pairing up with someone already addicted. They really don't know how to have fun.

When a client has difficulty making up a fun list, I start him off by asking him to make a list of things that he thinks might be fun. Then, over a period of a few weeks, he experiments with sampling these different activities. Remember that this is generally a slow process; it takes time for someone to learn how to have a good time, particularly when he has never had any experience doing it.

Over the years, I have had the opportunity to work with many recovering alcoholics who are now alcoholism counselors. One of the first things that I suggest when working with a professional is that he or she make a fun list. Almost always, quite bit of time has passed since the last experience of these activities. It is also surprising how many counselors include "work" on their list of fun things. This may be true, but if it's all the enjoyment the counselor has going on in his or her life, beware. This counselor may be in for a relapse and return to active alcoholism.

Why don't you, the reader, try making a fun list. Right now. Take a pencil and write down three fun things that you love to do, and the date you did each last. If it's been a while since the last time you did EACH of the three things, you might think about taking a vacation. At the least, you might make a determined effort to start reintegrating these things into your life. Having fun is vital to well-being.

There is a saying that goes, "If you want something done,

ask a busy person to do it." A busy person can always find time to do one more thing. I have found this to be true, not only in my own life, but also in the lives of my clients. Activities seem to creep into our lives and mysteriously multiply.

For this reason, it is important to find out about all of the activities in which your client is involved. Many times, when a client has a feeling of being overwhelmed by life, there is good reason for him to feel overwhelmed—he may simply be doing too much! Alcoholics, in their first few years of sobriety, have a tendency to become involved in many different activities, and their involvement in these activities sometimes gets out of control. Then they resolve this uncomfortable feeling by adding more activities, which makes their lives feel more out of control. This process goes on and on.

I counseled with a woman who told me she could not seem to relax. She said she felt nervous most of the time and that she was having trouble sleeping. After we had talked for a while, I asked her to make a list of all her activities. Her list looked something like this:

Working a full-time job.

Parenting a three-year-old child.

Going to five or six A.A. meetings a week.

Being involved in a relationship.

Sponsoring five new people in A.A.

Volunteering at the local mental health center.

Being the secretary of a local civic group.

Working in her local community group.

Doing volunteer work at the women's center.

Exercising at the health spa.

Taking evening college classes.

This woman was simply amazed to see, in writing, so many activities. Until she took the time to stop and write her daily experiences in a list, she had no real idea of how full her life had become. One by one, over a period of time, she had added so many activities to her life that she was becoming extremely uncomfortable.

Her next step was to prioritize her involvements and gradually to stop doing the things that were least important to her. After she had done this, she calmed down, became less nervous, and stopped having trouble sleeping. She, like many newly-sober people, had had difficulty saying no when asked to do things. Now, after making and prioritizing the above list, she no longer felt an obligation to do all that she was asked to do.

I recommend to my clients that they periodically take the time to list all the activities in which they are involved. This activities list is an effective positioning tool to help the client become aware of what he is actually doing with his time. This positioning can help to keep him from becoming overwhelmed by activities that creep into his life unnoticed.

Many times a client will have difficulty in prioritizing his list. When this happens, I ask the client to imagine that he knows he is going to die in one week; using this information about his death, I ask him to prioritize his list, placing at the top of the list those activities that are most meaningful to him.

Clients invariably respond with answers such as, "I would spend more time with my family;" "I would tell my mother I love her;" "I would be kinder to my husband." This method helps the client to focus on what really is of value to him. With this awareness, the client can begin to reintegrate into his life those activities that are of real value.

It is important to find out who your client relates to, as well as the activities which he enjoys. Who are the significant others in his life? Who are the people he can really talk to?

Many of my clients tell me that they have "lots" of people that they can talk to, and this may very well be true. These people, however, are of little value to the client if he does not really talk to them. There is a great deal of difference between having a lot of people to talk to and really talking to them. Potentially, we can talk to the whole human race; this potential, for the most part, however, goes unrealized.

It is important to identify the quality of the conversations that your clients are having.

During a counseling session with a client named Tom, I asked him if he had a support group of people that he could talk to. His reply was, "Yes, of course I do." He had his family, his co-workers, and the members of his A.A. group. He said that he had plenty of people in his life that he could talk to.

I asked Tom to list six people with whom he felt he could really discuss any major subject, and requested he focus on subjects such as sex, relationship conflicts, employment problems, things that made him feel fearful and guilty, and his day-to-day living problems.

Tom could not come up with six people that he could talk to about these subjects. After some effort, he did come up with two names. When I asked Tom the date when he last had a meaningful conversation with either of these two people, he could not even remember.

Tom is very typical of a person who easily gets lost in the crowd. He was surrounded by persons with whom he could potentially talk, but he never did, except in safe generalities. By the time Tom came to see me, he was feeling isolated and lonely; he couldn't understand why he felt so alone. His view of himself, that he had a good support group of people with whom he regularly shared, was not substantiated in reality.

At one time, Tom had used his support group, but over the years of his sobriety, he'd stopped using them. He became caught up in listening to other people talk to him about their problems, and he slowly stopped talking about himself and his problems. He became unwilling to let people know that he had problems, that he needed to share his feelings.

Listing his support group and dating as the last times he spoke with anyone on the list was an important process for Tom. By seeing the list, Tom realized that he was living in a fantasy; with the knowledge that he gained from the positioning list, he renewed his commitment to speaking, in depth, to the people in his support system. He also agreed to make an effort to add some new people to his support system.

I suggest my clients ask themselves positioning questions throughout their day. These questions help them to get a position on "right now," so they don't get stuck in a feeling, thought, or behavior that will cause them pain. The questions are:

1. What am I feeling right now?

2. What am I thinking about right now?

3. What am I doing right now?

These are important facts to know. Unfortunately, as the movement of the day progresses, most of my clients forget to ask the questions. To bring the positioning questions back into their conscious minds, I ask them to write the questions down and carry them somewhere on their persons, generally some place that they refer to often (with their change, keys, or cigarettes, for instance). When they reach for an item and come up with the list of positioning questions, they have the opportunity to stop and take stock of what is going on, at that moment, in their lives.

The three questions position the client in three of the four dimensions of existence. (The fourth dimension is the all-encompassing dimension of the spirit.) These are:

1. The emotional dimension (what am I feeling right now).

2. The mental dimension (what am I thinking right now).

3. The physical dimension (what am I doing right now).

When a client becomes aware of what he is doing in these three dimensions, he can then change. Awareness is critical; without the awareness of what is going on with him, the client will remain "stuck," not knowing why he is feeling, thinking, or acting the way he is. With awareness can come acceptance; the client can then begin to let go of his painful feelings, irrational thoughts, and potentially-damaging behavior.

Some clients wish to become involved in positioning themselves in the spiritual dimension. If a client wishes to do this, develop a positioning statement, with him, that is in keeping with his or her spiritual beliefs. It is important to involve your client in the development of this statement; this will avoid inadvertently pushing your spiritual beliefs onto your client.

These positioning statements will help your client realize a sense of what is happening in his or her "here and now." With this realization, your client can begin the process of acceptance and change which is a necessary part of growth.

By acquainting our clients with these simple positioning techniques, we can assist them in focusing on a clearer picture of what is going on in their lives. Many recovered alcoholics and addicts lose their sense of perspective; they get all wrapped up in doing the everyday tasks of living and allow the fun and joy to slip out of their lives. When we can help our clients to recapture this sense of fun and joy, and give them tools that will help them to live in the present moment, in today, then we have truly given them a gift.

Breathing

When a child is born, one of its first acts of independence is to breathe. The child's diaphragm contracts, and his lungs fill with life-giving air, which is then exhaled (sometimes with a cry). This process of inhalation and exhalation is continued throughout life, and is one of the last acts that is taken before death. To breathe is to live.

Most of us know that if we stop breathing for any length of time, death will occur, or the brain will sustain damage that will affect a person's mental and physical faculties. This is common knowledge. What is not common knowledge is that the way that we breathe can have a direct effect on the quality of life that we live.

Our breath is our connection to life. Every minute we breathe approximately 20 times. Although breathing is something that we do constantly, awake or asleep, most of us are unaware of our breathing; we take it for granted. Even now, as you read this, I would guess that there are some who are wondering why I am stating the obvious. They know that breathing is important; what they don't know is the effective breathing can alter the way a person relates to the world.

The alcoholic client has, over the course of his life, learned to breathe in an unhealthy way. If you observe your clients' breath processes, you will notice that most of them breathe shallowly and irregularly. This is not surprising. Shallow and uneven breathing is characteristic of the "flight or fight" state of mind and emotions associated with alcoholics. The alcoholic has spent a number of years in high-stress situations, and his natural stance is always to be on guard, poised, ready to flee or to defend. Active alcoholism forces a person to live this way. Along with other stress symptoms that accompany the flight or fight syndrome (i.e., fear, anxiety, rapid heart rate), shallow, uneven breathing is usually present. Over the years, this type of breathing becomes a habit to the alcoholic.

Even after the drinking has stopped, this kind of breathing usually continues. The way a person breathes affects his emotional and physical state, and the shallow, rapid breathing of the flight or fight syndrome can itself cause anxiety or stress. This cycle will continue over and over. A simple way to assist your client to break out of this unhealthy cycle is to teach him how to breathe in a more effective way.

Most people breathe by using their chest muscles; their chests generally rise and fall with their breaths. Chest breathing is just the opposite of the way babies and children breathe. If you watch a sleeping baby, you can see that his stomach rises and falls with each breath, not his chest. The child naturally uses his diaphragm to breathe, and diaphragmatic breathing is the most efficient way to breathe, both for children and adults.

The diaphragm, which is positioned between the lungs and stomach, is the muscle that expands and contracts when one is breathing correctly. To determine whether your client is breathing diaphragmatically, have him place one hand just below his rib cage, above his stomach. Then ask to him take a deep breath. Observe whether his hand moves in or out. Does it move at all? If he is breathing effectively, his hand will move out when he inhales.

Most of the time, you client's hand either will not move at all, or will move inward when he takes a deep breath. This is not surprising, when you consider that most people are taught to hold their stomachs in and their chests out. Unfortunately, this posture inhibits healthy breathing.

You can teach your client diaphragmatic breathing by having him place his hand between the bottom of his rib cage and his navel. As he takes a deep breath, have him push his hand outward with his stomach. As his diaphragm contracts, it will move downward, pushing out the stomach and creating a vacuum in the lungs into which the air rushes. Thus, the client's hand will move outward when he is breathing diphragmatically.

Diaphragmatic breathing is healthier in part because the largest amount of blood circulates in the lower sections of the lungs. When breathing diaphragmatically, oxygen is drawn down into these lower sections of the lungs and the vital oxygen/carbon dioxide exchange that takes place is much more effective. The person who is breathing diaphragmatically is providing his body with much more oxygen.

Breathing is both a simple and a complicated process. It is simple because it is something that we all do all the time. It is as simple as "taking a breath." Breathing, on the other hand, is a complicated process, because there are very sophisticated biological and chemical exchanges that take place during the act of breathing.

And while it is important to teach your client to breathe deeply and diaphragmatically, it is also important to teach him to breathe evenly. Uneven and ragged breathing is a sign of distress. The sob of grief, startled gasp, and the deep, forceful breaths of anger are all signs that a person is in some degree of distress or emotional turmoil. These situations are not necessarily negative, but it is unhealthy to continue to breathe in a shallow, ragged manner after the situation that caused the distress has resolved itself.

Deep breathing is an excellent relaxation method your clients can use regularly in stressful situations. During the early stages of recovery, many alcoholics will respond to different kinds of situations with anger, fear, rage, and hysteria. Their responses are responses that have been pre-programmed into the unconscious, and in many cases the client is as afraid of his response to a situation as he is of the situation itself.

Learning to control his breathing during stressful situations will help your client to become calmer and more relaxed. This lessening of emotional turmoil will provide the client with an opportunity to be able to think and make choices in situations that formerly might have overwhelmed him with fear and anger.

One of my clients became panicked whenever she had to speak in public. Before speaking, her breath would become shallow and ragged, and she would be filled with fear. To help her overcome this, I taught her to use deep breathing before speaking. After doing this a number of times, she became less and less panicked when she spoke in front of a group of people.

As a crisis counselor in the emergency room of a hospital, I used deep breathing with patients many times. When people are frightened and in pain, their breathing becomes shallow and uneven. In order to help these patients deal with their crises, which could be anything from the death of a loved one to free-floating anxiety, I would simply help them to breathe diaphragmatically throughout their crisis phase. I also used this technique myself, whenever I felt my own breathing become stilted or erratic, so I could function as a counselor in a calmer and more effective way.

There are two basic exercises that I use when I am teaching diaphragmatic breathing.

Exercise One

Have the client sit in an upright position, with his back straight. Ask him to picture his lungs divided into three parts—a lower, a middle, and an upper part. Have him take a deep, even, continuous breath, and visualize the lower portion of his lungs filling with air; then the middle section of his lungs filling with air; last, the upper part of his lungs filling with air. During this breathing process, ask him to be aware that as he is breathing into his lower lungs, his diaphragm is contracting and is pushing his stomach slightly outward. When the middle section is filling with air, have him be aware that his chest is expanding slightly. When he is breathing into his upper lungs, suggest he be aware that his shoulders are raising a small amount. When he exhales, have him visualize the air leaving the top part of his lungs first, then the middle part, and then the lower part, until all of the air is expelled from his lungs.

When all of the air is expelled from his lungs, ask him to become aware of how it feels for his lungs to be empty. Suggest that he pause for a moment, between exhaling and inhaling, and rest.

Then repeat the process of inhaling and exhaling. Do this for ten cycles of breathing in and out.

Throughout this exercise ask your client to try to breathe through his nose. Many people are not used to doing this and it may seem uncomfortable at first, but the exercise is most effective when breathing through the nose.

A variation on the above exercise is to have your client lie on his back and do the same breathing exercise. When doing the exercise in this position, have the client hold his hands on his diaphragm so he can feel his stomch moving up and down as he breathes. This will help those who have trouble moving their stomachs when they breathe in a sitting or standing position.

When your client has practiced doing the above exercise and feels comfortable doing diaphragmatic breathing, let him know that it is appropriate to do this type of breathing at any time during the day, not just when things get stressful. Deep breathing can and should be done 30 to 40 times per day (one deep breath each time). Pick times with your client when deep breathing would be both convenient and beneficial. Some of these occasions might be when he looks at the clock, answers the telephone, is stopped at a red light, stalled in traffic, etc. Be creative with your ideas.

Exercise Two

Have the client do the same type of inhalation as in Exercise One, filling his lungs from the lower portion to the upper. When he exhales, have him exhale completely and sigh audibly while he is exhaling. This is the well-known "sigh of relief." The sigh of relief is effective in letting go of tension and anxiety. At first your client may be embarrassed to "sigh" in front of you; if so, ask him to try doing this exercise at home. It will do wonders to help him relax and let go of tension.

Many recovering alcoholics and addicts smoke cigarettes. This does not mean that they cannot participate in these breathing exercises. In fact, it is important that they do. Diaphragmatic breathing can assist them in getting much-needed oxygen to parts of the body that are oxygen deficient because of smoking. When doing the above exercises with heavy smokers, warn them that they may feel a little light-headed during, and for a short period after, the exercise. This is due to the fact that they are not used to getting that much oxygen into their systems.

Breathing plays a crucial role in maintaining the integrity of the human organism. We can help our clients to learn to let go of old habits of breathing that are unhealthy, and to learn to breathe in a way that is healthy. Breathing, done correctly, can help the client generate more vitality and alertness. It can help him to relax and let go of stress and tension. To breathe is to live; to breathe fully and deeply is to live fully and deeply. The gift of breath is a gift of life.

A final thought . . .

There is one gift that I have not, as yet, discussed in this book. Without this gift, all of the other tools and techniques that have been discussed are diminished. This is the gift of love, the unconditional love that forms the bond between the counselor and the client. If love is absent from the counseling relationship, then all of the learned tools and techniques in the world will be of little consequence.

The gifts that we have discussed in the preceding pages can assist the client to look inside himself and explore those inner landscapes of being that exist in each one of us. Discovery of self-love and self-acceptance is one of the results of this journey of self-exploration. To assist our clients in this process, we, as counselors, must first love and accept ourselves. I truly believe that we cannot give away what we do not already possess ourselves. We cannot teach from ignorance.

Please take the gifts that I have shared with you in this book and try them yourselves. I acquired all of the information that is contained within these pages from others who were willing to share with me. I share these gifts with you, so that you may use them, if you wish, and pass them on to your clients, the alcoholic and his family members who are trying to lift themselves from a world of fear, pain, and darkness into a place of love, joy, sunlight, and recovery.

Reference Bibliography

Davis, Roy. **An Easy Guide to Meditation.** Georgia: CSA Press, 1978.

Denning, M. and Phillips, O. **The Llewellyn Practical Guide to Creative Visualization.** Minnesota: Llewellyn Publications, 1981.

Gawain, Shakti. **Creative Visualization.** New York: Bantam Books, 1982.

Levine, Stephen. **A Gradual Awakening.** New York: Anchor Books, 1979.

Mason, L. **Guide to Stress Reduction.** California: Peace Press, 1979.

Progoff, Ira. **At A Journal Workshop.** New York: Dialogue House Library, 1975.

Ram Dass. **The Journey of Awakening.** New York: Bantam Books, 1978.

Ray, Sondra. **I Deserve Love.** California: Les Femmes Publishing, 1976.

Silverstein, Lee. **Consider the Alternatives.** Minnesota: CompCare Publications, 1977.

Simon, Sidney B.; Howe, Leland W., and Kirschenbaum, Howard. **Values Clarification.** New York: Hart Publishing Company, Inc. 1972.

Small, Jacquelyn. **Transformers: The Therapists of the Future.** Florida: Health Communications, Inc. 1982.

Smith, Maury. **A Practical Guide to Value Clarification.** California: University Associates, 1977.

Swami Rama; Ballentine, R. and Haymes, A. **Science of Breath.** Pennsylvania: The Himalayan International Institute of Yoga Science and Philosophy, 1979.